WILL YOU TAKE ME?

Train up a child series

Jessica Hernandez

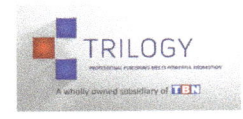

Trilogy Christian Publishers
A Wholly Owned Subsidary of Trinity Broadcasting Network
2442 Michelle Drive
Tustin, CA 92780

Cover design by: Cornerstone Creative Solutions

For information, address Trilogy Christian Publishing
Rights Department, 2442 Michelle Drive, Tustin, Ca 92780.
Trilogy Christian Publishing/ TBN and colophon are trademarks of Trinity Broadcasting Network.

For information about special discounts for bulk purchases, please contact Trilogy Christian Publishing.

Manufactured in the United States of America

10 9 8 7 6 5 4 3 2 1

Library of Congress Cataloging-in-Publication Data is available.

ISBN 978-1-63769-868-6 (Print Book)
ISBN 978-1-63769-869-3 (ebook)

Son, may this be a reminder to follow your dreams. I believe in you.

Take me to that place...

Where we get to have fun.

Take me to that place...

Where I get to see my friends.

Take me to that place…

Where we get to sing, dance, and clap those beautiful songs that make me smile.

Take me to that place...

Where we get to cut and paste, color, and play games.

Take me to that place...

Where I get excited to be there.

Take me to that place...

Where we learn about that man who died
for me.

13

Take me to that place...

Where we learn to say, "I am sorry."

Take me to that place...

Where I feel love, joy, and peace.

Take me to that place...

Where my tears fall down when I am happy.

Take me to that place...

Where I laugh all the time.

Take me to that place…

Where I asked Jesus in my heart.

23

"Mommy, it's time to wake up."

Notes from the Author

This book is for children and parents. It is a simple reminder of the importance of attending service. It is a simple guide a child can use to lead them toward salvation or a parent's guide to lead their child toward salvation. May this book be a reminder of the joy you feel when entering into God's presence in the point of view of a child. At the end, it shows the struggle parents feel on Sunday mornings, but our purpose means so much more.

CPSIA information can be obtained
at www.ICGtesting.com
Printed in the USA
LVHW071623110422
715897LV00021B/713